LAUGHING Lungs

and the respiratory system

JOURNEY THROUGH the **Human BODY**

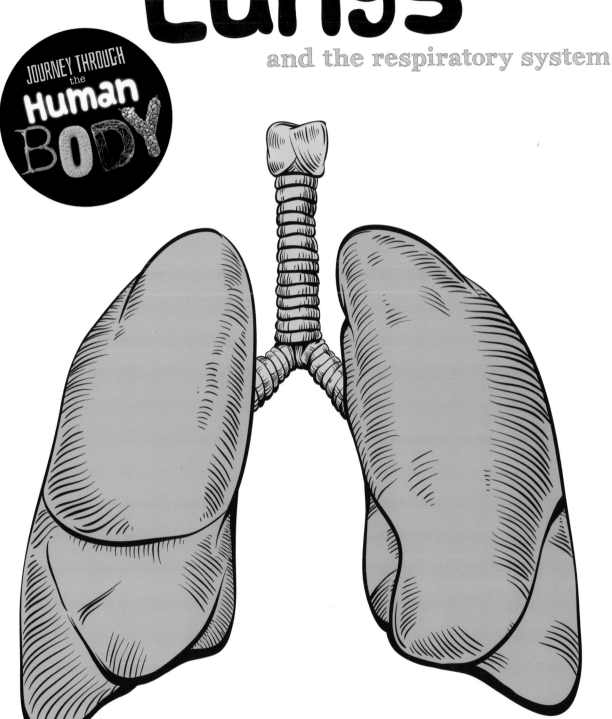

By Charlie Ogden

Designed by Danielle Jones

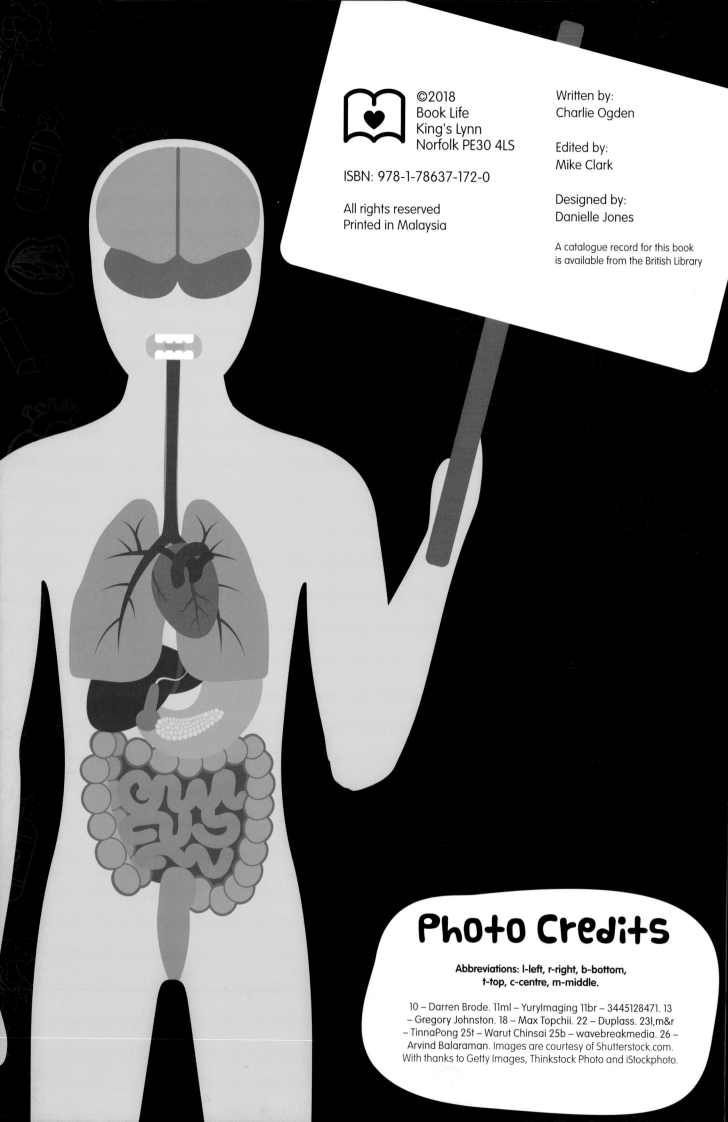

©2018
Book Life
King's Lynn
Norfolk PE30 4LS

ISBN: 978-1-78637-172-0

Written by:
Charlie Ogden

Edited by:
Mike Clark

Designed by:
Danielle Jones

A catalogue record for this book
is available from the British Library

PHoto Credits

**Abbreviations: l-left, r-right, b-bottom,
t-top, c-centre, m-middle.**

LAUGHING Lungs
and the respiratory system

CONTENTS

$$C + O_2 \rightarrow CO_2$$

Words that look like **this** are explained in the glossary on page 31.

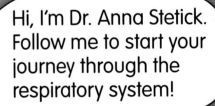

Hi, I'm Dr. Anna Stetick. Follow me to start your journey through the respiratory system!

The HUMAN BODY

The human body is very complicated. The body is full of **organs**, bones, **muscles** and **blood** and all of these parts are wrapped up in a thin layer of skin. Because of this, finding your way around the human body can be very difficult and dangerous if you don't have a guide.

But lucky for you, I am here – so let our journey begin!

There are over **75 ORGANS** in the **HUMAN BODY!**

SYSTEMS OF THE BODY

The first thing that you need to know about the body is that it uses **systems**. The systems of the body are made up of groups of organs that work together.

Each system of the body has its own important job to do, such as stopping the body from getting sick or helping to keep the body strong.

There are lots of different systems in the body, but some are more important than others. Four of the most important systems in the body are:

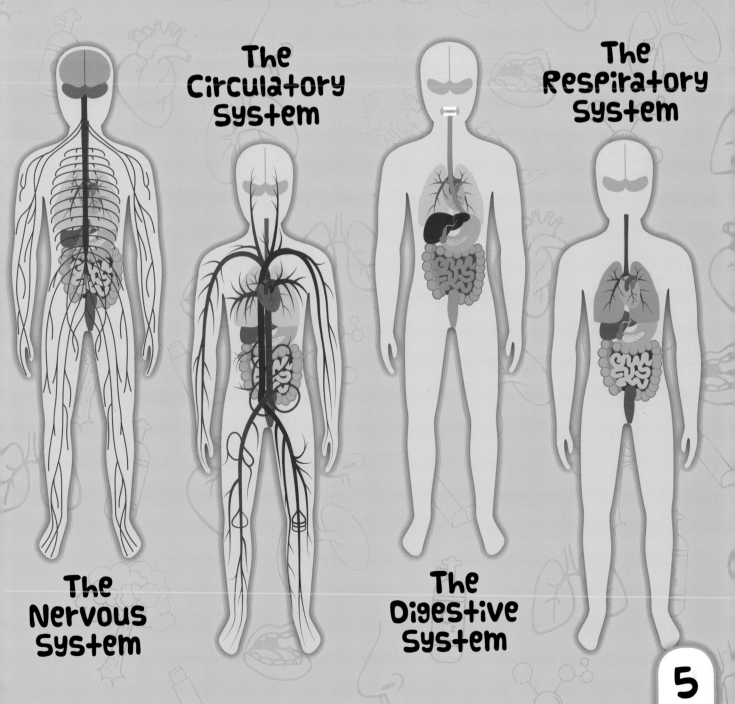

The Circulatory System

The Respiratory System

The Nervous System

The Digestive System

The RESPIRATORY SYSTEM

There are a few basic things that the human body needs to survive. These include food, water and, most importantly, oxygen! Oxygen is one of the **gases** that makes up the air that we breathe.

The body can survive for three weeks without food and for three days without water, but it would barely last three minutes without oxygen. The respiratory system is the group of muscles and organs in the body that allow you to breathe and take in oxygen from the air.

3
Weeks

3
Days

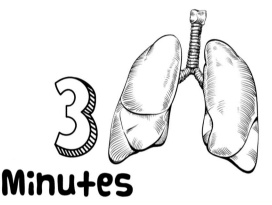

3
Minutes

THERE'S SOMETHING IN THE AIR...

The body gets the oxygen that it needs from the air. However, the air hasn't only got oxygen in it. In fact, most of the air around us is made up of nitrogen gas, but our bodies do not need this gas to survive.

This diagram shows all the different gases that make up the air.

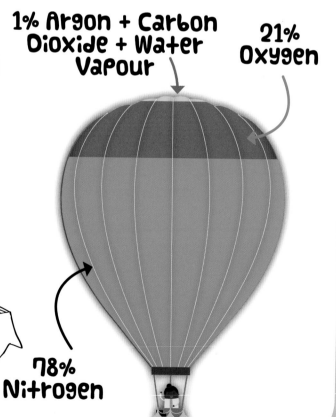

1% Argon + Carbon Dioxide + Water Vapour

21% Oxygen

78% Nitrogen

A BREATH OF FRESH AIR

The main job of the respiratory system is to get oxygen out of the air so that it can be used by the body. There is no other way for oxygen to get into the human body, meaning that you could not survive without your respiratory system!

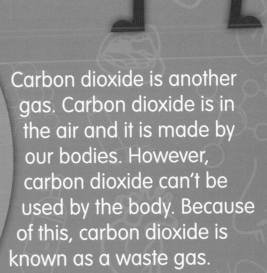

1% Argon +
Water Vapour

5% Carbon
Dioxide

16%
Oxygen

78%
Nitrogen

Carbon dioxide is another gas. Carbon dioxide is in the air and it is made by our bodies. However, carbon dioxide can't be used by the body. Because of this, carbon dioxide is known as a waste gas.

The second job of the respiratory system is to get rid of the carbon dioxide gas that builds up in the body. When you breathe out, carbon dioxide from the body gets released into the air.

We breathe out more carbon dioxide than we breathe in. This is because the body produces carbon dioxide as it uses up oxygen.

REQUIRED to RESPIRE

Oxygen is very important for the body. It helps to give it **energy**. Oxygen is used by every organ and muscle in the body. This means that without oxygen, no part of the body would be able to carry on doing its job.

As the body uses up oxygen, it produces the waste gas carbon dioxide. Too much carbon dioxide can be dangerous, even deadly. This is why it is so important that the body uses the respiratory system to get rid of it. With each breath you take, you are taking in oxygen and releasing carbon dioxide.

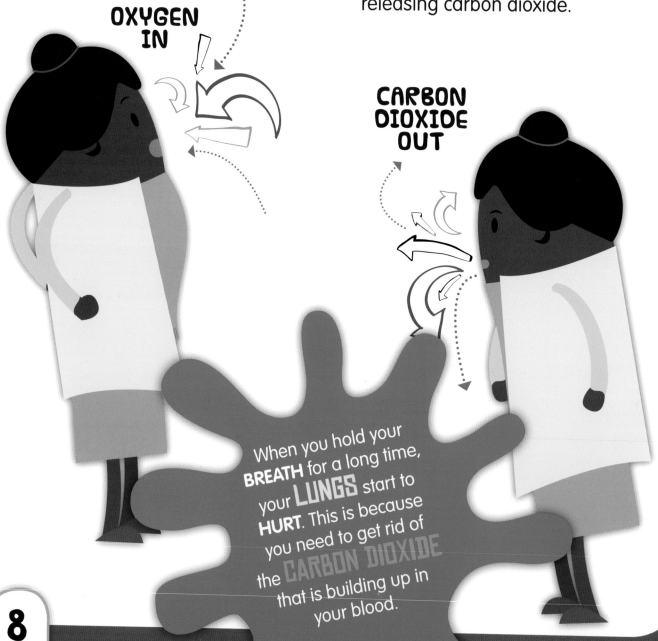

OXYGEN IN

CARBON DIOXIDE OUT

When you hold your **BREATH** for a long time, your **LUNGS** start to **HURT**. This is because you need to get rid of the CARBON DIOXIDE that is building up in your blood.

ORGAN-ISATION

The **LEFT LUNG** is always slightly smaller than the **RIGHT LUNG**. This is to make **EXTRA SPACE** for the **HEART** to fit into the chest.

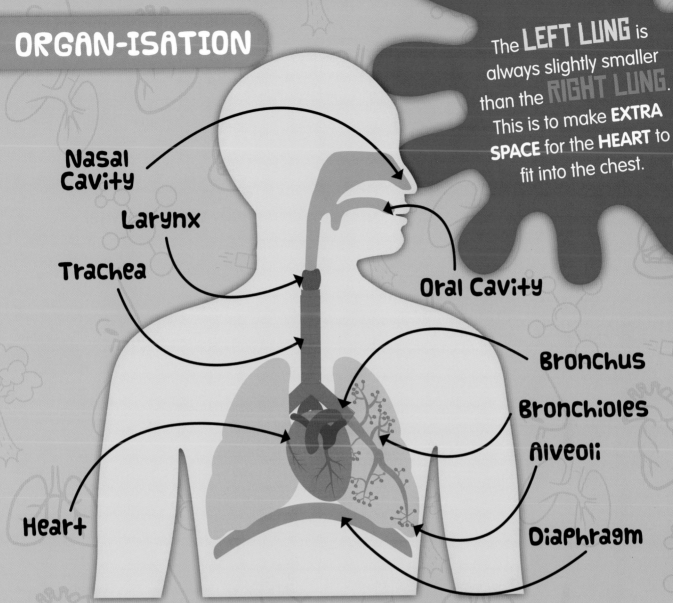

Nasal Cavity

Larynx

Trachea

Oral Cavity

Bronchus

Bronchioles

Alveoli

Heart

Diaphragm

The respiratory system has lots of different parts to it. The main organs in the respiratory system are the lungs. However, while the lungs are very important, they need help from a lot of different organs and muscles in order to do their job. Without the other parts of the respiratory system, the lungs would be useless.

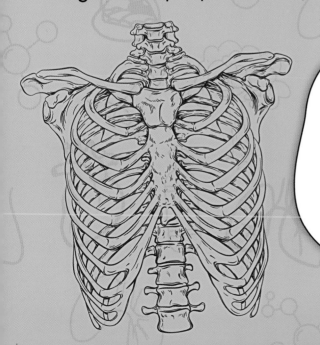

Another part of the body that is important to the respiratory system, but which isn't an organ, is the rib cage. This is a collection of bones that helps to protect the lungs and heart from damage. The muscles around the rib cage also help with breathing.

A MATTER of LIFE and BREATH

Breathing seems like a very simple thing – we breathe in and we breathe out. We've been breathing since the moment we were born and we breathe all day, every day. However, the respiratory system is actually very complicated and it involves a lot of different organs and muscles.

A person's respiratory system is strongest when they are between 25 and 30 years old.

Most of the systems in the body work automatically. This means that the systems do their jobs without you having to think about it. For example, the heart pumps blood, the stomach **digests** food and the brain feels pain, all while you do absolutely nothing.

Time	Number of Breaths
1 Minute	16
1 Hour	960
1 Day	23,000
1 Year	8,400,000
1 Lifetime	600,000,000

AUTOMATIC

A baby's first breath can be very difficult as their lungs have to fill with air for the very first time. Before this, a baby's lungs are filled with **fluid**.

Other parts of the human body do not work automatically. Instead, we have to make them do things ourselves. When people walk around, carry things or talk out loud, they decide to make these things happen themselves.

The respiratory system is a little bit different from these other systems. A lot of the time, breathing is automatic. This is especially true when people are sleeping – a person's breathing rate changes a lot when they are sleeping, but they never know about it.

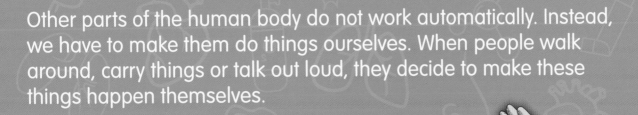

NON-AUTOMATIC

When a person is sleeping, their breathing is automatic.

However, there are other times when breathing is non-automatic. People can hold their breath if they want to and stop themselves from breathing. This is not something that you can do with your heartbeat. Very few systems in the body can be both automatic and non-automatic, which makes the respiratory system very special.

When a person blows out birthday candles, their breathing is non-automatic.

DEEP IN THE DIAPHRAGM

Even though the lungs are the most important part of the respiratory system, they do not actually help with breathing. The lungs do not suck air into the body or push it out again. Instead, this job is done by the diaphragm.

The diaphragm is one of the most important muscles in the body. Not only does it help the body to breathe, but it also separates the **abdomen** from the **chest cavity**. This means that it separates the organs that mostly deal with digestion from the organs that mostly deal with respiration and blood **circulation**.

The diaphragm sits just under the lungs and stretches all the way across the body. The diaphragm, being a muscle, can contract and relax. When muscles contract, they squeeze together and become tight, but when they relax, they become loose and soft.

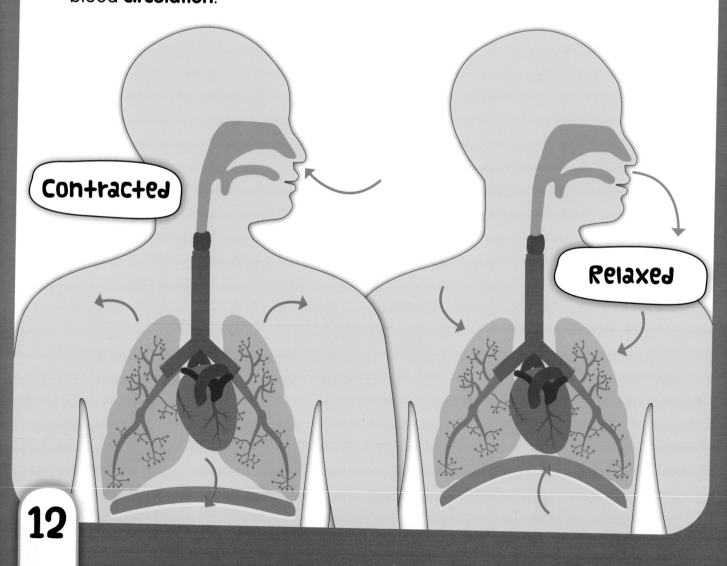

Contracted

Relaxed

When the diaphragm is relaxed, it bends upwards and makes an umbrella shape. When it contracts, however, the centre of the diaphragm gets pulled down. This increases the size of the chest cavity and makes air rush into the lungs.

When the diaphragm relaxes, the lungs can spring back to their normal size. This pushes air back out of the lungs.

When you force the air out of your lungs, like when blowing up a balloon, muscles inside your ribcage contract. This makes the chest cavity smaller and forces air out of the lungs quickly.

The diaphragm does the same thing as pulling on this handle. It makes the chest bigger, which draws air into the lungs.

Look out for these signs. The pink section shows you where we are in the body!

HICCOUGHS, or **HICCUPS**, are caused by **spasms** in the **DIAPHRAGM**. The diaphragm **SQUEEZES** together very quickly and this causes air to **RUSH** into the lungs.

BREATHE Down Your NECK

There are two main stages to breathing; breathing in (which is also called inhaling) and breathing out (which is also called exhaling). When the body inhales, the diaphragm and the muscles in the chest contract, making the chest cavity expand. This causes air to rush in through the mouth and nose.

The nasal cavity, oral cavity and trachea are all warm and wet. This makes the air warm and **moist** as it travels to the lungs, which helps to make sure that the lungs do not dry out.

Your TRACHEA and lungs can sometimes **HURT** when you do **exercise** in cold weather. This is because the air is very **COLD** and dry.

The nasal cavity and the other nasal airways are covered in lots of tiny hairs. They are also coated in a thin layer of sticky **mucus**. Mucus is mostly made of water, but it also contains a mixture of other things that help to protect the respiratory system. Mucus in the respiratory system is known as phlegm.

Although the hair and mucus in the nasal cavity have lots of jobs, their main job is to filter the air that is breathed in through the nose. Small bits of dust, dirt and other things that float around in the air get trapped in the hairs and mucus in the nose. This stops them from getting into the lungs and causing damage.

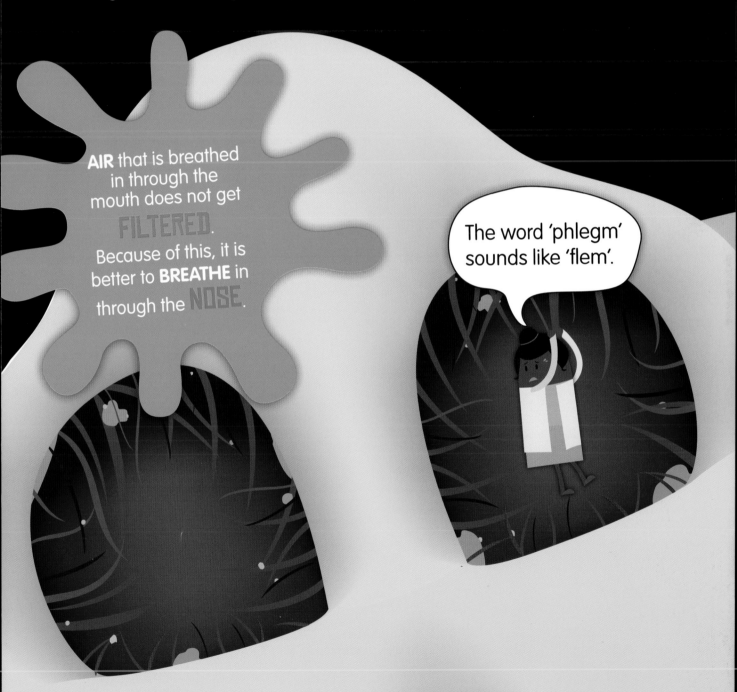

AIR that is breathed in through the mouth does not get FILTERED. Because of this, it is better to **BREATHE** in through the NOSE.

The word 'phlegm' sounds like 'flem'.

LAUGHING Lungs

When air reaches the end of the trachea and is about to enter the lungs, it flows either into the right bronchus or the left bronchus. Air that flows into the right bronchus fills up the right lung and air that flows into the left bronchus fills up the left lung.

The LEFT LUNG only has TWO lobes because it is SMALLER than the RIGHT LUNG.

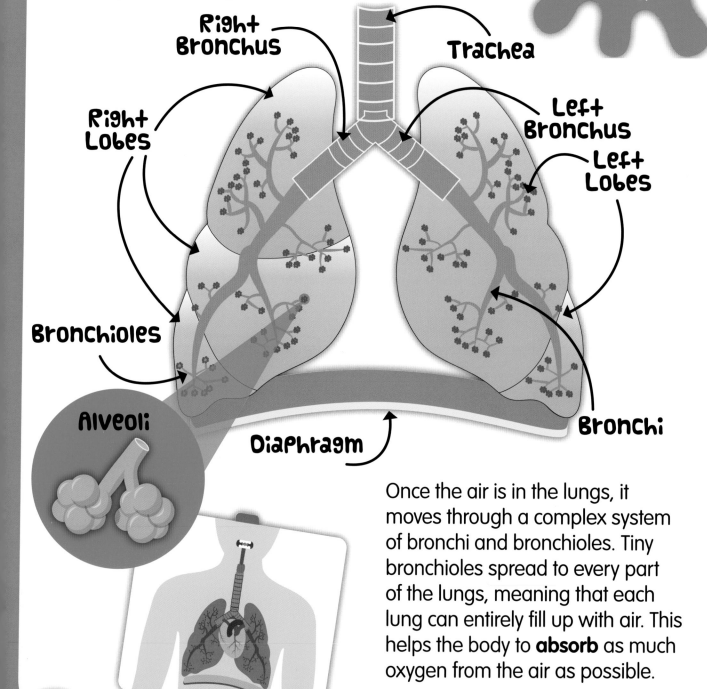

Right Bronchus

Trachea

Right Lobes

Left Bronchus

Left Lobes

Bronchioles

Alveoli

Diaphragm

Bronchi

Once the air is in the lungs, it moves through a complex system of bronchi and bronchioles. Tiny bronchioles spread to every part of the lungs, meaning that each lung can entirely fill up with air. This helps the body to **absorb** as much oxygen from the air as possible.

The lungs are very spongy and springy. This helps the lungs to stretch when air is inhaled and to return to their normal shape when air is exhaled.

However, the lungs being spongy also has another purpose – it makes it so that there are more places where oxygen can be absorbed into the body.

Lungs need to be big enough to take in lots of oxygen, but still small enough to fit inside the chest. Because of this, our lungs are squished up like springs.

Imagine these two lines are the inside of your lungs. The blue dots show where oxygen is being absorbed into the lungs. As you can see, both lines can absorb the same amount of oxygen, but line one takes up a lot less space than line two. In this example, line one is like the lungs – it takes in lots of oxygen but doesn't take up much space!

1.

2.

ALVEOLI ACTION

The most important things in the lungs are probably the alveoli. This is where oxygen is absorbed into the body and carbon dioxide is taken out of the body.

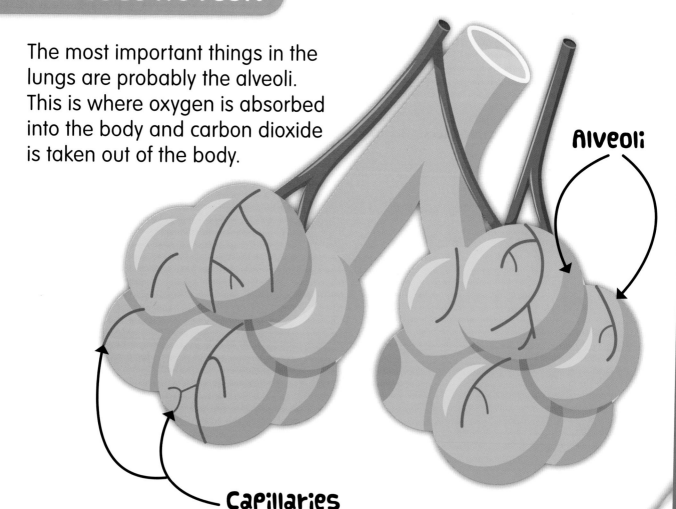

Alveoli

Capillaries

Alveoli can be found at the end of bronchioles and they are covered in tiny **blood vessels** known as capillaries. At the end of each bronchiole is one alveolus. There are around 300 million alveoli in each lung and each one is about 0.2 millimetres across. That's 50 times smaller than a pea!

Inside each alveolus, oxygen from the air is swapped with carbon dioxide from the blood. The blood in the capillaries around the alveoli is not like the rest of the blood in the body. This blood has lots of carbon dioxide in it and almost no oxygen. This is the opposite of what the body needs.

The air in the alveoli, however, is very different. It has lots of oxygen in it and much less carbon dioxide than the blood does. Because of this, carbon dioxide from the blood goes into the alveolus and oxygen from the alveolus goes into the blood. Now the alveolus and the capillary both contain similar levels of oxygen and carbon dioxide. The blood is now said to be oxygenated because it contains lots of oxygen.

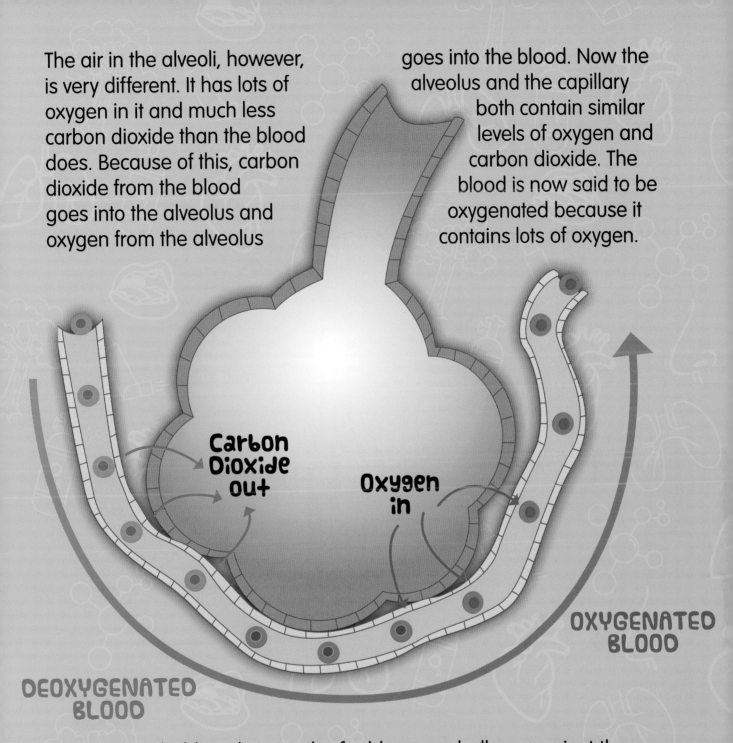

Carbon Dioxide out

Oxygen in

OXYGENATED BLOOD

DEOXYGENATED BLOOD

Think about holding the mouth of a blown-up balloon against the mouth of a balloon that hasn't been blown up. Imagine that you could hold them together so perfectly that no air would escape. What do you think would happen?

The air would not all rush from one balloon to the other. Instead, half of the air from the first balloon would rush into the second balloon, meaning that both balloons would be blown up the same amount.

In the same way, all the oxygen in the lungs doesn't rush into the blood. Instead, it balances out so that both the blood and the air in the alveolus have about the same amount of oxygen and carbon dioxide.

Happy HEART

Once the lungs have got oxygen into the blood, the blood needs to carry it to the rest of the body. As it does this, it picks up carbon dioxide from the body and takes it back to the lungs to be breathed out. These are the two main jobs of the circulatory system, which is made up of the heart and lots of different blood vessels.

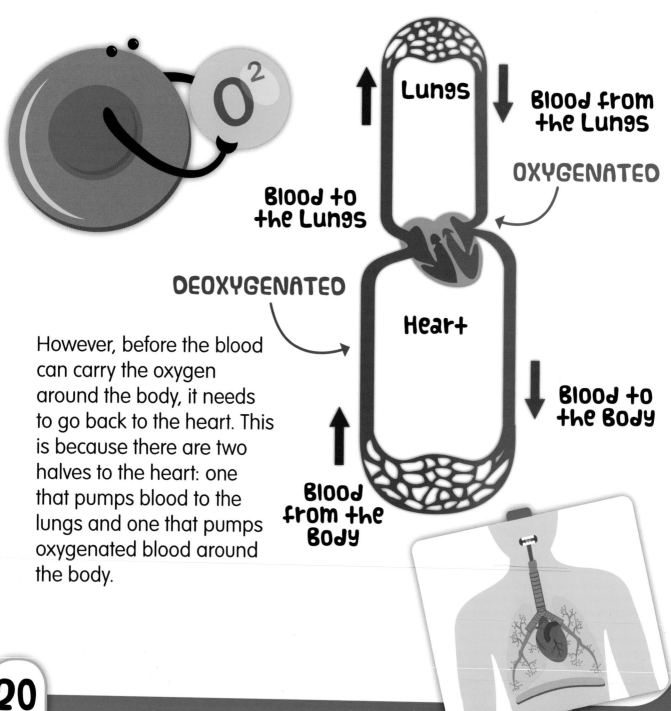

Lungs

Blood from the Lungs

OXYGENATED

Blood to the Lungs

DEOXYGENATED

Heart

Blood to the Body

Blood from the Body

However, before the blood can carry the oxygen around the body, it needs to go back to the heart. This is because there are two halves to the heart: one that pumps blood to the lungs and one that pumps oxygenated blood around the body.

Once the oxygenated blood has made it to the heart, it is ready to make its journey around the body. By the time it gets back to the heart, the blood will be deoxygenated, meaning that it will have used up all of its oxygen. It will then need to be pumped back to the lungs to pick up more.

The circulatory system uses three main types of blood vessel to transport blood around the body: arteries, capillaries and veins. Arteries travel away from the heart, meaning that they take oxygenated blood to the different muscles and organs in the body.

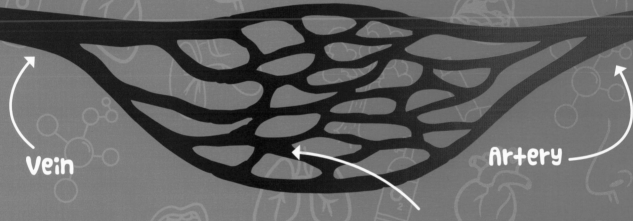

Vein

Artery

Capillary

As they get farther away from the heart, the arteries get smaller and smaller until they become capillaries. Capillaries are so small that they can stretch to every part of the body. It is in the capillaries that oxygen in the blood is swapped for carbon dioxide made by the body. After this, the capillaries join together and get bigger and bigger until they turn into veins. Veins take the deoxygenated blood back the heart.

If you laid out all of the **BLOOD VESSELS** in the human body in a line, it would **REACH AROUND THE EARTH TWO AND A HALF TIMES**.

Ready, Set, BREATHE

Doing lots of exercise makes you breathe much faster. This is because the body needs more energy than usual when it does exercise and oxygen helps to give the body energy.

16 Breaths Per Minute

While Resting

50 Breaths Per Minute

While Exercising

When the body is resting, each breath takes in about half a litre of air. When the body is exercising, each breath can take in as much as three litres of air.

3 litres

0.5 litres

Breathing more quickly helps to get more oxygen into the body. It also helps to remove more carbon dioxide from the body. Because the body uses more oxygen when it is exercising, it also produces more carbon dioxide.

AEROBIC VS ANAEROBIC

So far we have only looked at normal, aerobic respiration. This is when oxygen in the blood is used to give the body energy. However, this isn't the only type of respiration. When the body does lots of exercise and the lungs cannot breathe fast enough to get the right amount of oxygen into the body, the body starts doing something known as anaerobic respiration.

Anaerobic respiration doesn't need any oxygen to work. Instead, it only needs some of the **glucose** that gets into your body through the food you eat. However, it does have some downsides. Whereas aerobic respiration produces carbon dioxide (and some water), anaerobic respiration produces lactic acid. Lactic acid can cause pain in your muscles. This is why you sometimes get a painful stitch in your side after running around a lot.

You **BREATHE HEAVILY** even after finishing exercise because your body needs **OXYGEN** to turn the **LACTIC ACID** in your body into carbon dioxide and water.

SAVE YOUR VOICE

We now know that the respiratory system is very important. However, there's more! As well as giving the body all the oxygen it needs, the respiratory system also helps us to speak, shout, sing, laugh and whisper.

Larynx

When Breathing

When Talking

Near the top of the trachea is an organ called the larynx. Inside the larynx are the vocal folds, which are also known as the vocal cords. These are two pieces of **tissue** that stretch across the larynx.

When we breathe, the vocal folds pull back to open up the larynx and allow air through. But when we want to talk, sing or shout, the vocal folds stretch over the larynx and close most of it off.

The **LARYNX** is also sometimes called the **VOICE BOX**.

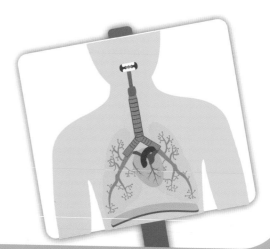

SAY 'AHHH'

When the vocal folds are stretched across the larynx and air from the lungs is forced between them, they vibrate and make a sound.

If the vocal folds are only loosely stretched across the larynx, they will make a sound with a low **pitch**. If the vocal folds are tightly stretched across the larynx, they will make a sound with a high pitch.

Articulator(s) Used	Sounds
Lips	'b', 'm' and 'p'
Teeth	'c' and 'j'
Tongue	'l'
Lips and Teeth	'f' and 'v'
Teeth and Tongue	'n' and 'th'

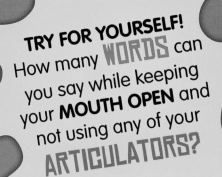

TRY FOR YOURSELF!
How many **WORDS** can you say while keeping your **MOUTH OPEN** and not using any of your **ARTICULATORS?**

This is as much as the vocal cords can do – if you want to turn these sounds into actual words, you need to use your articulators.

The articulators are the parts of the mouth, throat and nose that help people to turn sounds into words. The tongue, teeth, lips and nasal cavity are all articulators. Without all of these things, we would not be able to speak.

SAVE your BREATH

There are a number of different things that can affect the respiratory system, making it more difficult to breathe and get oxygen into the body.

ASTHMA

Asthma is a **disease** that affects the lungs and respiratory system. You cannot catch asthma. Instead, most people find out that they have asthma when they are very young. Between 5% and 10% of people have asthma, making it one of the most common diseases to affect the respiratory system. Most people with asthma live normal lives. However, if someone with asthma has an asthma attack, it can be very scary.

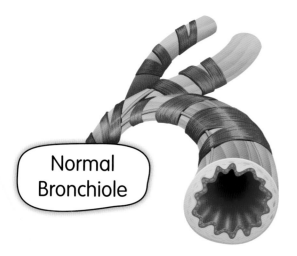

Normal Bronchiole

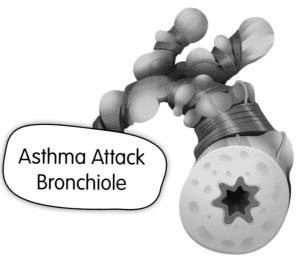

Asthma Attack Bronchiole

When someone with asthma has an asthma attack, their trachea, bronchi and bronchioles become **inflamed** and swell up. They also begin to fill with mucus. These two things can make it very difficult to breathe, which is why having an asthma attack can be so scary. Inhalers help to make the lungs less inflamed and to reduce swelling, making it easier to breathe again.

SMOKING

Smoking cigarettes is one of the most damaging things that a person can do to their lungs. Smoking has been proven to lead to numerous health problems and it causes over 5,000,000 deaths around the world each year.

When people smoke cigarettes, harmful chemicals in the smoke damage their trachea, bronchi and bronchioles. This causes mucus to build up in the lungs, making it harder to breathe. This is why people who smoke often have a cough.

Even just being around people who are smoking can damage your lungs, especially if you have a lung disease such as asthma.

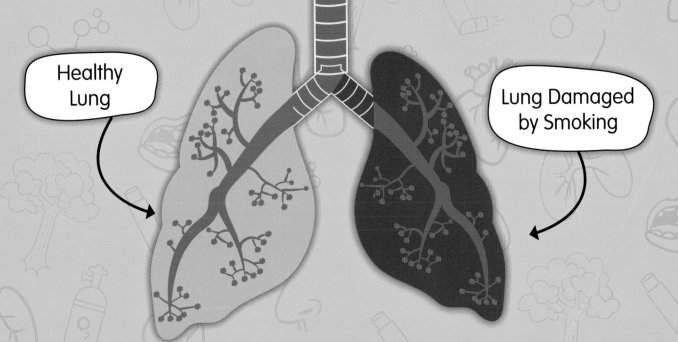

Healthy Lung

Lung Damaged by Smoking

Smoking also makes it harder for the alveoli to exchange oxygen in the air with carbon dioxide in the blood. If someone smokes for a long time, their lungs can get so full of mucus that they can't take in as much oxygen as a person with healthy lungs. This can make breathing very difficult for them. They will also be more likely to develop serious health problems.

27

RESPIRATION
Information

1. Thousands of years ago in ancient Greece, asthma was treated by drinking a mixture of wine and owl's blood.

2. The world record for the longest amount of time that someone has held their breath is 22 minutes.

3. If your lungs were completely flattened out, including all the alveoli, they would be the same size as a tennis court.

4. The average person breathes in about 550 litres of oxygen every day. That's about the same as four bathtubs full of oxygen.

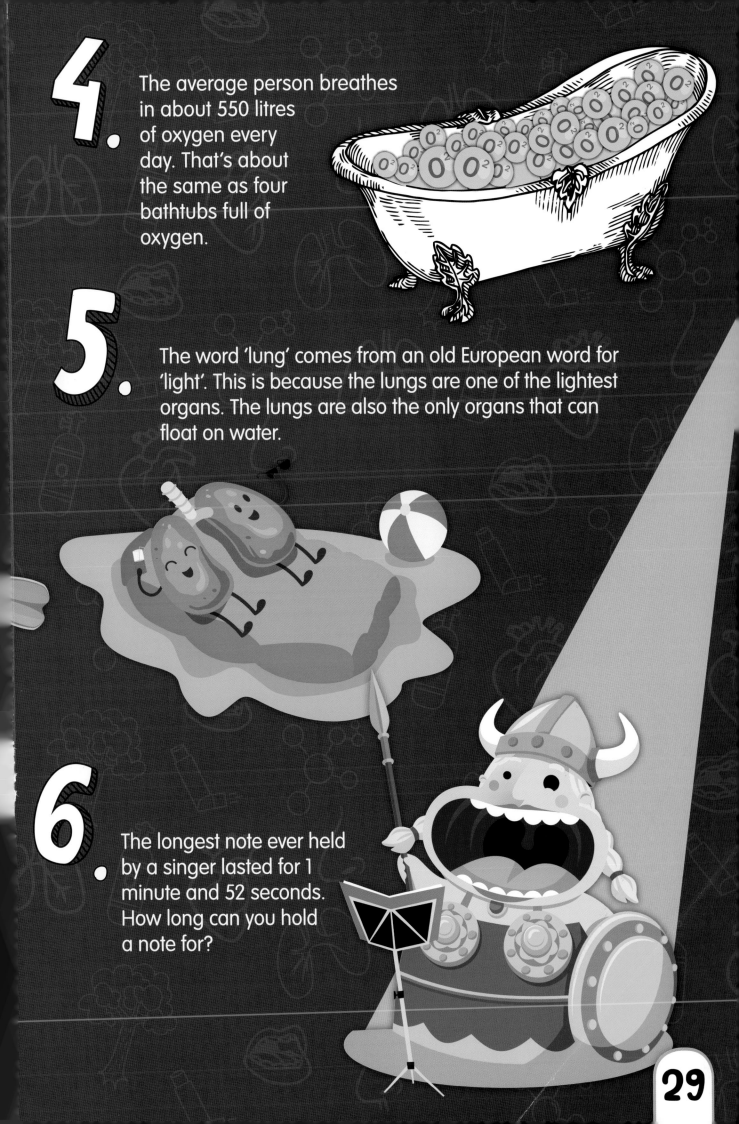

5. The word 'lung' comes from an old European word for 'light'. This is because the lungs are one of the lightest organs. The lungs are also the only organs that can float on water.

6. The longest note ever held by a singer lasted for 1 minute and 52 seconds. How long can you hold a note for?

Test in your CHEST

Use what you've just learnt to try to answer these questions. The answers are upside down at the bottom of the page.

1. What is the name for the parts of the body that allow us to turn sounds into words?

2. What is another name for the larynx?

3. What waste gas is produced as the body uses up oxygen?

4. What muscle sits underneath the chest cavity and helps with breathing?

5. About how many breaths does a person take each day?

6. When we are sleeping, is our breathing automatic or non-automatic?

7. What is the name for mucus that is in the respiratory system?

8. Which lung is smaller, the right or the left?

9. What does anaerobic respiration produce instead of carbon dioxide and water?

10. What is at the end of the bronchioles in the lungs?

Answers: 1. Articulators 2. Voice Box 3. Carbon Dioxide 4. Diaphragm 5. 23,000 6. Automatic 7. Phlegm 8. Left 9. Lactic Acid 10. Alveoli!

GLOSSARY

abdomen	the part of the body that contains the digestive organs
absorb	to take in or soak up
blood	the red liquid that circulates through the body and carries oxygen and carbon dioxide
blood vessels	tubes in the body that blood flows through
chest cavity	the part of the body that is protected by the rib cage and holds the lungs and heart
circulation	the continuous movement of blood through the body
digests	breaks down food into things that can be absorbed and used by the body
energy	the strength needed for physical and mental activity
exercise	activities that require physical effort
fluid	a substance that flows, especially a liquid
gases	air-like substances that expand freely to fill any space available
glucose	a simple sugar that is an important energy source in living organisms
inflamed	swollen and sore
lobes	round and flat parts of something, which often hang down or project out
moist	slightly wet
mucus	a slimy substance that helps to protect and lubricate certain parts of the human body
muscles	bundles of tissue that can contract or squeeze together
organs	parts of the body that have their own specific jobs or functions
pitch	how high or low a sound is
spasms	sudden, involuntary muscle contractions
systems	sets of things that work together to do specific jobs
tissue	any material that a living thing is made out of, including humans

INDEX